Summary of

The Innovators

by Walter Isaacson

Instaread

Please Note

This is an unofficial summary.

Table of Contents

Book Overview

The Innovators by Walter Isaacson is a detailed and comprehensive guide to the people who contributed to the digital revolution. The history that leads up to the present-day computer and the Internet age began with Ada Lovelace, the daughter of the poet Lord Byron. In 1843, Ada Lovelace wrote a scientific paper describing a machine that Charles Babbage proposed. Although his Analytical Engine was never built, Ada Lovelace's description covered four main concepts that are embodied in modern-day computers although they were not invented until a century after her notes were written. She described a multi-purpose machine that could process and act upon anything that could be expressed in symbols. This machine could be given instructions on what to do by way of a sequence of operations. She also made clear that the machine would never be able to think on its own. It would only be able to do what it was instructed to do.

It would be a hundred years before technology would advance enough to create a working model similar to Babbage and Lovelace's idea of a computer. However, several innovations paved the way. One of the most notable of these was in 1890 when Herman Hollerith created tabulator machines that made use of electrical circuits to process information. He went on to establish the company now known as International Business Machines Corporation (IBM).

Major technological developments occurred in 1937 that define modern computers. As a result of these innovations, computers were defined as being digital, on a binary system, electronic, and multi-purpose. Many people are credited with bringing about these innovations, including Alan Turing, Claude Shannon, George Stibitz, Howard Aiken, Konrad Zuse, and John Vincent Atanasoff. John Mauchly and J. Presper Eckert are credited with inventing the Electronic Numerical Integrator and Computer (ENIAC) in 1943, the first electronic general-purpose programmable computer. It became the model for all subsequent computers.

When it came to programming computers, women played a very important, but little-known part. Grace Hopper was a programming pioneer. She could easily translate scientific problems into mathematical equations and then into English. She wrote what was to become the first computer programming manual. Jean Jennings and five other women were chosen to work on the programming for the ENIAC.

Early computers used expensive vacuum tubes, but the invention of the transistor brought about a revolutionary change. Walter Brattain, John Bardeen, and William Shockley, three men who worked together at Bell Labs, are credited with the invention of the transistor.

The next major innovation was the invention of the microchip. This happened independently in two places by Jack Kilby, who worked for Texas Instruments, and by Robert Noyce, who worked at Fairchild Semiconductor. Noyce's version could be efficiently mass-produced, so his design became the model for the future.

Additional developments led to the invention and popularity of video games. This began with *Spacewar*, which was created by Steve Russell, and *Pong*, which was developed by Nolan Bushnell. Bushnell started the video game company Atari.

Vannevar Bush, creator of the Differential Analyzer, was the person most responsible for bringing together the three groups that formed a partnership to create the Internet. Collaboration between the military, universities, and private corporations allowed the formation of the Internet, a network that encouraged time-sharing, real-time interaction, and interfaces that made easier the man-machine connection. Once again, the work of many people brought about change. Joseph Robnett Carl Licklider, John McCarthy, Bob Taylor, Larry Roberts, Paul Baran, Donald Davies, Robert Kahn, and Vint Cerf all made unique contributions that helped to make the Internet a reality.

The personal computer was first built by Alan Kay, Butler Lampson, and Chuck Thacker called the Xerox Alto, but Xerox did not market it. Next, Ed Roberts and his friend Forrest Mims created a do-it-yourself kit for a rudimentary computer called the Altair 8800. Paul Allen and Bill Gates set out to create software for the Altair 8800 so that hobbyists could create their own programs on it. Allen and Gates formed their own software company and called it Microsoft. Microsoft Beginner's All-purpose Symbolic Instruction Code (BASIC) became the industry standard, and Microsoft software dominated the software industry for more than thirty years. Steve Wozniak and Steve Jobs formed a company called Apple and built the Apple I and Apple II personal computers. The Apple II was the first home computer that was simple and fully integrated with a screen and keyboard.

Additional technological advancements further revolutionized the digital age. Ray Tomlinson invented email when he devised a system of messaging that used the "@" symbol to instruct a message to go to a certain file folder. Online communities came into being that offered bulletin boards, discussion groups, consumer-oriented services, chat rooms, and instant messaging. Al Gore supported the National Information Infrastructure Act of 1993 which made the Internet widely available to the general public. Tim Berners-Lee, with the help of his project manager, Robert Cailliau, created the World Wide Web. Marc Andreessen created the Mosaic browser. The Blogger site was launched by Ev Williams. Wikipedia, an online encyclopedia, was created, and Google, a high-quality search engine, was established.

Just as Ada Lovelace envisioned, the programmable general-purpose computer came true. Additionally, artificial intelligence has not materialized. Computers have not taken the place of humans, but they have become partners with them. Personal computers combined with the Internet have brought about content sharing, online communities, digital creativity, and social networking on a grand scale.

The revolution of the digital age has shown that creativity is a collaborative process and that innovation is more likely to happen when a team is involved. Most of the entrepreneurs and innovators who brought about the digital age were people who cared about and understood the design and engineering of a product.

Important People

Ada Lovelace: Ada Lovelace, the daughter of poet Lord Byron, believed in Charles Babbage's concept for a machine that he wished to create called the Analytical Engine. She wrote a scientific paper about it, describing it as a multi-purpose machine that could process or act on anything that could be expressed in symbols and that could follow instructions given to it in the form of a sequence of operations.

Vannevar Bush: Vannevar Bush was an Massachusetts Institute of Technology (MIT) engineering professor who linked together multiple integrators in 1931 to create a machine he called a Differential Analyzer. This was the world's first analog electrical-mechanical computer.

John Mauchly: John Mauchly teamed up with J. Presper Eckert to build the first electronic, general-purpose computer. It was given the name Electronic Numerical Integrator and Computer or ENIAC, and it became the model for most computers that followed.

J. Presper Eckert: J. Presper Eckert was an engineering expert who worked as a partner to John Mauchly. Together they invented the ENIAC computer which was electronic, general-purpose, and programmable.

Robert Noyce: Robert Noyce was one of the traitorous eight who left William Shockley's company and formed their own company known as Fairchild Semiconductor. He designed the microchip which was practical and could be mass-produced efficiently.

Ted Hoff: Ted Hoff and his team at Intel created a general-purpose chip that could be programmed to do a variety of applications. This new device was called a microprocessor, and it made possible personal computers for the home.

Bill Gates: Bill Gates teamed up with Paul Allen to form the computer software company Microsoft. Microsoft's operating system software dominated the software industry for more than thirty years.

Steve Jobs: Steve Jobs worked for Atari before joining with Steve Wozniak to form Apple, Incorporated. Jobs and Wozniak worked together to create the Apple II personal computer which came already assembled, was simple to use, and was fully integrated.

Steve Wozniak: Steve Wozniak partnered with Steve Jobs to form the Apple company. Wozniak designed the Apple I computer by integrating a microprocessor, screen, and keyboard, and Steve Jobs convinced him to market it.

Tim Berners-Lee: Tim Berners-Lee collaborated with Robert Cailliau to create the World Wide Web. His vision was to have all the information stored on computers everywhere linked in a web that was free, openly shared, and in the public domain.

Thank you for purchasing this Instaread book

Download the Instaread mobile app to get
unlimited text & audio summaries
of bestselling books.

Visit Instaread.co
to learn more.

Chapter Summaries & Key Takeaways

Introduction

Most important inventions and innovations that have to do with the digital world in our era did not come about because of the lone efforts of individuals. Instead, they came about as a result of the collaboration of many people. Creativity was increased as a result of these collaborations. Social and cultural forces also provided the proper background for innovation.

Personal computers were designed as tools for the individual to use creatively. The Internet was created to make collaboration easier. The combination of the two in the late 1980s led to the current digital revolution. These innovations made it possible for anyone anywhere to create, share, and access information.

The creative collaboration that created the digital age involved both peers and innovations made in earlier generations. The digital age also created a partnership between computers and their users. Those who made the

[handwritten marginalia: collaboration and creativity led to the invention of technology that would increase both]

liberal arts experience

connection between art and science have had the most influence in the innovations of the digital age.

Key Takeaways

- Collaborative effort and shared creativity between many individuals combined with social and cultural forces inspired most of the important innovations and inventions of the digital age.

- The coming together of personal computers and the Internet in the late 1980s made it possible for anyone anywhere to create, share, and access information.

- Collaboration among peers, between generations, and between people and machines brought about the digital age. Those with the most influence in the digital age were those who believed in the importance of both art and science.

Chapter 1

Ada Byron, the daughter of poet Lord Byron, was tutored in math by her mother. As a result, she grew up comfortable with the combination of art and science. She met Charles Babbage, a science and math expert. Babbage demonstrated a model of a machine that he built called a Difference Engine that could solve polynomial equations.

Ada was inspired by Babbage's Difference Engine and decided to undertake advanced lessons in mathematics. Ada became interested in mechanical weaving looms that used punch cards to create patterns in fabric. She recognized the similarity between the looms and Babbage's Difference Engine. Ada married William King who became the Earl of Lovelace. This made her Ada, Countess of Lovelace, or more commonly, Ada Lovelace.

Babbage had an idea for another machine. He wanted to create a computer that could carry out different operations. He called his concept an Analytical Engine. Babbage wanted to use punch cards in his new machine similar to the ones used in looms.

Ada Lovelace believed in his idea and imagined that it might be used to process other symbolic notations such as for music and art in addition to numbers. From 1842 to 1843, she wrote a translation of notes written by a young military engineer about the Analytical Engine. Her notes became more famous than the engineer's original article.

Ada's notes covered four principles of historical significance. The first was that this would be a multi-purpose machine. The second was that it could process and act upon anything that could be expressed in symbols. The third was that the machine would work because of specific instructions given to it. Ada created this sequence of operations herself and wrote it up into a table and diagram. Her creation made her the world's first computer programmer. The fourth concept Ada wrote about was that computers could not think and could only perform as they were instructed. Babbage's machine was never built, and Ada never wrote another scientific paper, but their ideas were the beginnings of the digital age that came a century later.

Key Takeaways

- Ada Lovelace studied advanced math after being impressed by Charles Babbage's machine called the Difference Engine that could solve polynomial equations. He had ideas for another machine that he wanted to build that he called an Analytical Engine.

- Ada wrote up notes about the Analytical Engine that contained four historically significant concepts. These concepts were that the machine would be multi-purpose, that it could process anything that could be expressed in symbols, that it would work as a result of a sequence of operations, and that it would not be able to think on its own.

- Ada wrote the sequence of operations for Babbage's Analytical Engine into a table and diagram, making her the first computer programmer. Although Babbage's machine was never built, his ideas together with Ada's concepts were the beginnings of the digital age.

Chapter 2

In the 1890s, Herman Hollerith, an employee of the US Census Bureau, created tabulator machines to automate the census. This was "the first major use of electrical circuits to process information". (ch. 2, ePUB) He formed a company that eventually became the International Business Machines Corporation (IBM).

Vannevar Bush, a Massachusetts Institute of Technology (MIT) engineering professor, linked together multiple integrators in 1931 to build a device he called a Differential Analyzer. Bush's machine was analog, so it did not advance computer technology in an important way.

Major developments occurred in 1937 that were digital, on a binary system, electronic, and multi-purpose, four properties that defined modern computing.

The work of many people brought about these developments. Alan Turing envisioned a Logical Computing Machine that would use a binary system and perform actions based on instructions that it was given. Claude Shannon wrote an influential master's thesis that said complex mathematical problems could be solved by using a means of relay circuits. George Stibitz invented a Complex Number Calculator that showed how a circuit of relays could "do binary math, process information, and handle logical procedures". (ch. 2, ePUB) Howard Aiken created the Harvard Mark I as a modern version of Babbage's digital machine. German engineer, Konrad Zuse, created a binary calculator that received instructions from a type of data storage that used a long strip of paper with holes punched into it, punched tape. In 1939, John Vincent Atanasoff built a prototype of the first electronic digital computer and was almost finished with a full-scale model in 1942 when he was drafted into the Navy. His almost-working machine was stored in a basement and later dismantled.

America's entrance into World War II mobilized science at that time. John Mauchly teamed up with J. Presper Eckert, an engineering expert. Mauchly felt that the computer he was building with Eckert would help the Army. Their machine was given the name Electronic Numerical Integrator and Computer (ENIAC). ENIAC was digital but not binary. This made it different from a modern-day computer, but it was more advanced than previous machines. Another electronic computer, known as Colossus, was built by the British at the end of 1943, but few knew about it. It was all electronic and partially programmable, but it was not a general purpose computer. The ENIAC created by Mauchly and Eckert was the first to be general purpose as well as electronic and pro-grammable. It became the model for most computers that followed it.

Key Takeaways

- Herman Hollerith created tabulator machines to automate the census, the first major use of electrical circuits to process information. The company he formed eventually became known as IBM.

- Many major developments in the digital age occurred in 1937 brought about by many different people. Some of these people included Alan Turing, Claude Shannon, George Stibitz, Howard Aiken, Konrad Zuse, and John Vincent Atanasoff.

- John Mauchly and J. Presper Eckert, who built the ENIAC, are credited with inventing the first electronic, general-purpose programmable computer. It became the model for all subsequent computers.

Chapter 3

(handwritten marginal note: women in science (programming))

The next major step for the modern computer was storing programming inside a computer's memory. Grace Hopper was a programming pioneer. At different times she worked for Aiken, Eckert, and Mauchly. She could easily translate scientific problems into mathematical equations and then into English. This made her a good programmer. She wrote what was to become the first computer programming manual. Her programming was very systematic. She broke down each problem into small mathematical steps. She also perfected the subroutine, a set of instructions designed to execute a frequently used operation. Her work on the Harvard Mark I made it one of the most easily programmable computers at the time.

Jean Jennings was one of six women chosen to work on the programming for the ENIAC. The programming was crucial to the functioning of the computer. These six women developed the use of subroutines about the same time that Grace Hopper did.

Mauchly and Eckert realized that they needed to be able to store programs inside the computer's memory instead of loading them in every time. This would require a large memory capacity. They began working to develop this idea.

John von Neumann is mostly credited with the creation and improvement of the stored-program architecture that Mauchly and Eckert first had the idea to develop. Von Neumann became a consultant to the ENIAC team and thought the computer program should be stored in the same memory as the data. This would make it easy to modify as the computer was running.

A new and improved ENIAC was built that included much of the von Neumann architecture. It was known as the Electronic Discrete Variable Automatic Calculator (EDVAC). The work of von Neumann, Mauchly, and Eckert was again the same cooperative style of teamwork that helped to bring about the digital age⌐

Key Takeaways

- Grace Hopper worked as a programmer at different times for Aiken, Eckert, and Mauchly on the Harvard Mark I. She wrote what was to become the first computer programming manual and perfected the subroutine.

- John von Neumann is credited with creating and improving the stored-program architecture that was needed by Mauchly and Eckert.

- A new and improved ENIAC, known as the Discrete Variable Automatic Calculator (EDVAC), was built that included much of the von Neumann architecture.

Chapter 4

The first computers were costly machines because they relied on expensive vacuum tubes that used a lot of power. The invention of the transistor was a revolutionary change. Walter Brattain, John Bardeen, and William Shockley are credited with the invention of the transistor. These three all worked together at Bell Labs. Bell Labs was known for bringing together a variety of talent which brought about continued innovation. The key to innovation was to both nurture individual genius and promote collaborative team-work. Shockley was talented at visualizing quantum theory. Brattain was an avid experimenter. Bardeen was an additional theorist added to the team. Their mission was to create a replacement for the vacuum tube using semiconductors. Together they created the transistor, one of the most important discoveries of the twentieth century.

Innovation happens in stages. First there is the invention, then the production, and then the entrepreneurs who think up new markets and ways to use the product. Pat Haggerty was this type of entrepreneur. He came up with the idea of using transistors in a small pocket radio. It became one of the most popular new products in history. It was also an example of the desire to make devices personal, a theme that defines the digital age.

Shockley wanted to launch his own company to make transistors using gas diffusion. He wanted the company located in Palo Alto, helping to create what became known as Silicon Valley. Shockley hired Robert Noyce, Gordon Moore, and other talented employees. Shockley, unfortunately, was not a good leader. He was willful, demanding, and did not inspire loyalty. He was not good at sharing credit and had trouble creating a spirit of collaboration. As a result, Noyce, Moore, and six others made a pact to leave the firm and form a new company. Sherman Fairchild, the owner of Fairchild Camera and Instrument, became their corporate sponsor. These men became known as the traitorous eight. They formed Fairchild Semiconductor. Their timing could not have been better as the budding space program and the military ballistic missile program increased demand for both computers and transistors, tying together the development of these technologies.

Key Takeaways

- One of the most important discoveries of the twentieth century was the transistor. Walter Brattain, John Bardeen, and William Shockley are credited with its invention.

- Pat Haggerty was the entrepreneur who came up with the idea of using transistors in a small pocket radio which became one of the most popular new products in history. The desire to make devices personal is a theme that has come to define the digital age.

- William Shockley formed his own company making transistors in a new way. Robert Noyce, Gordon Moore, and six other employees of Shockey's company joined together to form their own company, Fairchild Semiconductor.

Chapter 5

Jack Kilby joined Texas Instruments in 1958. Kilby created the first microchip with his monolithic idea that combined several components in one monolithic piece of silicon, bypassing the traditional method of soldering them onto the circuit board. Texas Instruments called it a solid circuit.

Robert Noyce, at Fairchild Semiconductor, came up with the idea of a microchip independently a few months later. Noyce used the planar method of protecting delicate electrical parts from impurities to make multiple connections between transistors or other components on a single silicon chip. This version was more practical than Kilby's because it eliminated the excessive number of wires that would otherwise be sticking out.

Although Noyce's patent application was filed after Kilby's, it was ruled on first. As a result, Noyce was declared inventor of the microchip. The case went to court and eventually the decision was reversed and Kilby was declared as the inventor of the microchip. Fairchild appealed the case and the decision was again reversed. While the courts battled over the decision, Texas Instruments and Fairchild Semiconductor decided on their own to work things out and cross-licensed to each other whatever rights they had. Noyce's design could be mass-produced efficiently, so his version became the model for the future.

Noyce and Moore decided to form their own company. It was backed by venture capitalist, Arthur Rock, and was called Integrated Electronics Corporation which was shortened to Intel. With Intel came another innovation. It was the invention of a new corporate culture and management style. It was casual and averse to hierarchical distinctions. Both Noyce and Moore were unwilling to be bossy and did not have the ability to drive people. Andy Grove was hired as the director of engineering. His blunt management style was one of action that balanced out the laid back styles of Noyce and Moore.

Ted Hoff and his team at Intel created a component that was basically a general purpose computer on a chip. This new device was called a microprocessor. Microprocessors began showing up in many devices, but most importantly, they made personal computers for the home possible.

Key Takeaways

- Jack Kilby, who worked at Texas Instruments, and Robert Noyce, who worked at Fairchild Semiconductor, both came up with the idea of a microchip independently of each other in different ways. Noyce's version became the model for the future because it could be mass-produced efficiently.

- Noyce and Moore, along with Andy Grove, formed their own company with the support of venture capitalist Arthur Rock. Their company was called Integrated Electronics Corporation which was shortened to Intel.

Science meets business

- Ted Hoff and his team at Intel created the microprocessor. This invention made personal computers for the home possible.

Chapter 6

A student organization at MIT formed the Tech Model Railroad Club. Steve Russell, a programmer, was a member of the club. He and his friends decided to create a space-war game on a computer donated to the club by the Digital Equipment Corporation (DEC). When the basics were completed, the game *Spacewar* became an open-source project, making it available to other programmers to make changes and improvements as they saw fit. In this way, the game was greatly improved.

Alan Kotok and Bob Sanders, also members of the Tech Model Railroad Club, invented remote controls with which to play the game as a lasting contribution that carried over to the development of video games. The creation of the game *Spacewar* emphasized three aspects representative of the hacker culture. It was created collaboratively, it was free and open software, and it was based on the belief that computers should be personal and interactive.

Nolan Bushnell and his colleague, Ted Dabney, came up with the idea of turning a computer into an arcade video game. Bushnell's game was called *Computer Space*. For his next video game, Bushnell decided to start his own company, Atari. The game that Bushnell came up with was a computer version of Ping-Pong he called *Pong*. With his successful innovation, Bushnell became known as the man who launched the video game industry.

Corporate culture at Atari was similar to that at Intel. There was no dress code and no fixed working hours. It was all about creativity and a failure to conform to societal norms. This culture continued to help define Silicon Valley.

Key Takeaways

- Steve Russell, a member of the Tech Model Railroad Club at MIT, created the game *Spacewar*. Alan Kotok and Bob Sanders, also members of the Tech Model Railroad Club, invented remote controls to go with the game.

- Nolan Bushnell started his own company, Atari, and came up with a computer version of Ping-Pong that he called *Pong*. He became known as the one who launched the video game industry.

- Corporate culture at Atari continued to define Silicon Valley as a place where creativity was more important than anything else.

Chapter 7

The military, universities and private corporations were the three groups that built the Internet. Vannevar Bush, creator of the Differential Analyzer, was the person most responsible for bringing these groups together. Bush headed up the National Defense Research Committee and the Office of Scientific Research and Development. The Defense Department and the National Science Foundation were prime funders of much of America's basic research.

Joseph Carl Robnett Licklider was the originator of two important concepts that contributed to the formation of the Internet. Those two were decentralized networks that allowed the distribution of information to and from anywhere, and interfaces that enabled human to machine interaction in real time. He was also "the founding director of the military office that funded the Advanced Research Projects Agency Network (ARPANET)" (ch.7, ePUB). Licklider collaborated with John McCarthy to develop systems for computer time-sharing. He believed the best use of computer science was to create machines that worked well with human minds. He had a vision of what he called the Intergalactic Computer Network that would promote a connection between computers and their users as well as users around the world.

Bob Taylor came up with the idea of building a data network to connect research centers. A network funded by ARPA, the Advanced Research Projects Agency, did just this, allowing research centers to share resources and to work together on projects. Taylor hired Larry Roberts, a protégé of Licklider, to lead the project. In 1967, Roberts presented the plan for the network which he called ARPA Net. It was later changed to ARPANET.

Paul Baran helped the progress of the development of the Internet because of two key ideas he had. One idea was that control of the network should be completely distributed with no central hub. The other was to divide data into small, equally sized blocks. He fulfilled this second idea with the creation of packet switching. The work of Donald Davies in England also led him to the concept of packet switching.

Robert Kahn, along with his partner Vint Cerf, was determined to connect ARPANET with other packet networks into a system that was eventually called the internet. Unfortunately, use of the Internet was restricted to those with access to computers, mostly researchers within the military and universities. Personal computers were the next step to make the digital age truly transformational.

Key Takeaways

- The Internet came about because of a partnership between the military, universities and private corporations. Vannevar Bush was the person most responsible for bringing these groups together.

- Numerous people collaborated to bring about the creation of the Internet. Joseph Robnett

Carl Licklider, John McCarthy, Bob Taylor, Larry Roberts, Paul Baran, Donald Davies, Robert Kahn, and Vint Cerf all made unique contributions to make the Internet a reality.

- In the beginning, the Internet was primarily used by researchers at military and academic institutions. The personal home computer was the final innovation that would transform the world in the digital age.

Chapter 8

Stewart Brand realized that the combination of counter culture and cyber-culture was perfect for the digital revolution. Personal computers offered a valid opportunity for giving individuals power. He thought if people could see a photo of the earth from space that it would give them empathy for all others in the world and create a sense of connectedness. He convinced the National Aeronautics and Space Administration (NASA) to take such a picture and then used it on the cover of his venture, *The Whole Earth Catalog*. This catalog mixed traditional sensibilities with new advancements to suggest that people could enjoy technology and still be eco-friendly. This catalog laid the groundwork for the marketing of the personal computer.

Douglas Engelbart was an engineer who set out to find an easy way for humans to interact with machines. He wanted to find the simplest way for a computer user to point to and select something on a screen. The result of his research was the creation of the mouse. The mouse was one more step to make possible a personal computer that people could interact with in real time over a network that permitted collaborative creativity.

Alan Kay had a vision of small personal computers with graphic displays that would be simple enough for a child to use, inexpensive enough for everyone to own, yet powerful and well-equipped in order to promote personal creativity. Kay was hired at Xerox's Palo Alto Research Center (Xerox PARC). Kay pushed for the company to create a small, kid-friendly computer and call it the Dynabook, but his proposal was denied.

Two co-workers, Butler Lampson and Chuck Thacker, also wanted to build a personal computer. They joined resources with Kay and worked on creating the computer without permission. The machine they created was called the Xerox Alto. However, Xerox did not direct its sales toward private consumers, so it never became a leader in the field of personal computers.

Ed Roberts, a hobbyist, launched a company with his friend, Forrest Mims. Their company was called Micro Instrumentation and Telemetry Systems (MITS). They created a kit for a basic, inexpensive computer. The computer, named the Altair 8800, had no keyboard or other input device. The kit sold at a surprising speed, selling thousands in a matter of months. In this way, personal computers were taken from the control of the military and big corporations and put into the hands of individuals.

Key Takeaways

- Douglas Engelbart wanted to create the simplest way for a computer user to point to and select something on a screen. The result of his work was the invention of the computer mouse.

- Alan Kay, Butler Lampson, and Chuck Thacker worked together to create a personal computer called the Xerox Alto, but Xerox did not market it as a personal computer product.

- Ed Roberts and his friend, Forrest Mims, created a do-it-yourself kit for an inexpensive, rudimentary computer called the Altair 8800.

Chapter 9

When Paul Allen and Bill Gates were in college, the Altair 8800 came out. Allen and Gates set out to create software for the personal computer so that hobbyists could create their own programs on it. Their work launched the software industry for the personal computer. Monte Davidoff later became the third member of their team because he knew how to write the floating-point math routines that they needed. They were successful in creating a software program that ran on a home computer.

Allen and Gates went into the software business together and called their company Micro-Soft, which was later changed to Microsoft. Roberts took the Altair on a tour hoping to start fan clubs across the United States. Gates went along with him. During this tour, the punched paper tape that had the Beginner's All-purpose Symbolic Instruction Code (BASIC) program that Gates had written on it was borrowed and copies were made. From that, Microsoft BASIC was shared freely over and over. Gates was angered by this, but it helped his company in the end because it was so widely used, other companies had to pay to get access to it.

Gordon French held meetings of the Homebrew Computer Club in his garage. Steve Wozniak, a hardware engineer, was introduced to Steve Jobs, who lived a short distance away, at one of these meetings. They became friends and partners. Wozniak would come up with an engineering feat and Jobs would find a way to market it.

When Wozniak heard about the microprocessor through the Homebrew Computer Club, he realized he could use it to design a computer with a screen and keyboard integrated. In 1976, his design became the Apple I. Jobs convinced him that they should form a company together and market it. Jobs decided that the Apple II, the next computer they collaborated on, should come already assembled. Upon its release, the Apple II was the first truly user-friendly computer.

Dan Bricklin, Bob Frankston, and Dan Fylstra developed VisiCalc, the first financial spreadsheet program, to be used on the Apple II. Word-processing software, like Apple Writer and EasyWriter, came next.

At IBM, Bill Lowe was assigned the project of creating an IBM personal computer. Bill Gates was called in to help with the software, including an operating system. Gates and Allen bought the operating system software from a small company. This gave Microsoft the software that, after some improvements, dominated the software industry for more than thirty years. The IBM personal computer was introduced in August 1981.

Jef Raskin, an engineer for Apple, designed a computer that would eventually become the Macintosh. It included a graphical user interface that gave Apple an advantage over IBM computers with Microsoft software. However, in September 1981, Microsoft began work on the first version of their Windows operating system that also had a graphical user interface and could be used on IBM personal computers (PCs) and their clones. Eventually, Microsoft became the dominant company because they had a better business model.

Richard Stallman believed that software should be shared. The free and open-source software movement was strong because of the collaborative ethics in hacker culture. Stallman wanted to create a free operating system that was similar to and compatible with Bell Lab's UNIX. He called his system GNU, which was an abbreviation for GNU's Not UNIX. His system was missing the central module or kernel. Linus Torvalds supplied the kernel for the system that became known as Linux.

Key Takeaways

- Paul Allen and Bill Gates went into business together to create software for the personal computer and to form the company that came to be known as Microsoft. Microsoft BASIC became the industry standard, and Microsoft software dominated the software industry for more than thirty years.

- From the partnership between Steve Wozniak and Steve Jobs, the Apple I and then the Apple II were created. The Apple II was the first home computer that was simple and fully integrated with a screen and keyboard.

- The work of Richard Stallman and Linus Torvalds made the free and open-source software movement stronger with their creations of the GNU operating system and the Linux kernel.

Chapter 10

ARPANET was originally meant to aid in the sharing of computer resources, but it became a success when it was instead used for communications and social networking. Although electronic mail had been in use for some time, in 1971 Ray Tomlinson invented modern email. He used the "@" symbol that is now familiar to those in the digital age to instruct a message to go to a certain file folder. Email then became the main way of collaborating.

Early virtual communities were started with email chains on subscribed mailing lists. Some of the early virtual communities included Stewart Brand's The Well, an online community where users could discuss anything they wanted, William von Meister's The Source, a consumer-oriented online service, and Steve Case's America Online (AOL), that offered chat rooms, buddy lists, and instant messaging.

In 1993, government policies changed. This opened up the Internet to everyone. Senator Al Gore Jr. of Tennessee was the most influential person in this process. He helped promote the Information Superhighway. After being elected vice president, Gore supported the National Information Infrastructure Act of 1993. This made the Internet widely available to the public and brought a new era of growth to the economy.

science influenas America's economy.

Key Takeaways

- Ray Tomlinson invented email on ARPANET when he devised a system of messaging that used the "@" symbol to instruct a message to go to a certain file folder.

- Some early virtual communities included The Well, The Source, and America Online (AOL). These communities offered bulletin boards, discussion groups, consumer-oriented services, chat rooms, and instant messaging.

- Al Gore was the most influential person in support of the National Information Infrastructure Act of 1993. This act made the Internet widely available to the general public.

Chapter 11

In 1980, Tim Berners-Lee created a computer program called Enquire that was a catalog of the researchers, their projects, and their computer systems at the company, European Organization for Nuclear Research (CERN), where he was a consultant. While working on this, he had a bigger vision where he imagined all the information stored on computers everywhere being linked. He imagined forming a web of information. He came up with the idea of using hypertext, a word or phrase that links to another document or piece of content when the user clicks on it. He at first called the web address of a document a Universal Document Identifier. This was later changed to a Uniform Resource Locator (URL). He then created a Hypertext Transfer Protocol (HTTP) that allowed hypertext to be exchanged online, and Hypertext Markup Language (HTML) that was used to create pages. Berners-Lee needed a collaborator to make his ideas a reality. Robert Cailliau became the project manager to see the ideas through to completion. The project became known as the World Wide Web (WWW). Berners-Lee wanted the Web to be free, openly shared, and in the public domain. With its essence being the promotion of sharing and collaboration, the Web project was completed, allowing links to be made to any information anywhere.

In order to find sites on the Web, users needed a kind of software on their computers that became known as a browser. In 1993, Marc Andreessen created Mosaic, the first Web browser that had graphic capabilities and was easy-to-install.

In 1994, Justin Hall created a website called Justin's Links from the Underground, a directory to interesting links on the

Web. His Web Log also included information about his personal life and activities. As a result, Hall was credited with starting the very first Weblog. Later, Peter Merholz, a web designer, changed Web Log to We Blog. At that time the word blog became part of common vocabulary.

→ accessibility

Ev Williams created a blogger scripting tool that made blogging simple for everyone. He then launched the Blogger site in March of 2000. Blogger had 100,000 accounts by the end of that year. By giving people a simple way to publish on the Internet, Williams gave the public a voice. Williams also went on to be a cofounder of the social networking site, Twitter.

Additional developments were yet to come on the Web. Wiki software, which was developed by Ward Cunningham, allowed users to edit and contribute to a web page. Wikipedia, a creation of Larry Sanger and Jimmy Wales, is an online encyclopedia that was created collaboratively and maintained by volunteers. Wikipedia permitted people to share their own knowledge and have access to the knowledge of others. Google, a high-quality search engine, came to be as the result of work done by Larry Page and Sergey Brin. It became a simple human-computer network interface that helped people find what they needed.

Key Takeaways

- Tim Berners-Lee came up with the idea of using hypertext, set up the address of a document as the Uniform Resource Locator (URL), created HTTP, which allowed hypertext to be exchanged online, and created HTML, the language used to create pages. Then, with the help of his project manager, Robert Cailliau, he created the World Wide Web.

- Justin Hall is credited with writing the first blog. It began with his Web Log called Justin's Links from the Underground that included a directory to interesting links on the Web along with information about his personal life and activities.

- Many additional developments revolutionized the digital age. Some of these developments included the creation of the Mosaic browser by Marc Andreessen, the launch of Blogger by Ev Williams, the creation of Wikipedia, and the start of Google.

Chapter 12

Ada Lovelace would probably be pleased to know that the vision she and Charles Babbage had of a general-purpose computer came true. These machines appeared in the 1950s and two inventions revolutionized them. Microchips that permitted computers to become very small, and packet-switch networks that made computers capable of connecting on a web. Personal computers, combined with the Internet, brought about content sharing, online communities, digital creativity, and social networking on a grand scale.

Also, according to Ada Lovelace's prediction, artificial intelligence has not materialized. Computers today can store mass amounts of information and perform amazing numerical calculations, but they do not have many of the empathetic capabilities humans do.

Additionally, true to Ada Lovelace's intuition, computers have not replaced humans, but they have become their partners. It has been shown that computers can balance out human strengths and weaknesses. When they collaborate, they produce better results than when either works alone.

The revolution of the digital age has that innovation is more likely to happen when a team is involved. Also ideas were handed down from one generation to the next in addition to from peer to peer. The best technological teams were put together with people with a variety of special talents and complementary styles. The Internet also brought about collaboration within teams and from complete strangers.

There are three ways that the teams of innovators came together to create the digital revolution. First, government funding and coordination created teams. Then private enterprise built collaborative teams where creativity and invention were financially compensated. Finally, teams of independent hardware and software developers freely shared ideas among peers to expand on new ideas.

Many of the entrepreneurs and innovators who brought about the digital age were people who cared about and understood the design and engineering of a product. One other lesson learned from the digital age is that man is social. Nearly every digital tool created has been used for a social purpose.

One final point made by Ada Lovelace has also been shown to be true. The intersection of the arts with the sciences brings about the best results. The combination of the two cultures of technology and the humanities has brought about new forms of expression and new kinds of media, just as she envisioned.

Key Takeaways

- According to the predictions of Ada Lovelace, a multi-purpose computer has been created, artificial intelligence never really materialized, and computers have not replaced humans but have become partners to them. She was also right about the beauty and creativity that could come about by combining art with science.

- The digital revolution came about as a result of creative collaboration among peers on a team and from generation to generation. The best teams were made up of people with complementary styles, with a variety of special talents, and who cared about and understood the design and engineering of a product.

- Innovative teams were formed in three ways. These are government coordination and funding, through private enterprise, and by peers freely sharing ideas on a volunteer basis.

A Reader's Perspective

The Innovators: How a Group of Hackers, Geniuses, and Geeks Created the Digital Revolution by Walter Isaacson is a comprehensive, historical look at how technology has changed since the 1840s and how those changes brought about the digital age. This book provides bibliographic information about the who's who of inventors, visionaries, and entrepreneurs who gave the world the personal computer and other digital devices as well as the World Wide Web and the Internet.

A portrait of the personalities of these innovators is revealed through the course of the book. They had many things in common. They accomplished the most when they worked in collaboration with others who had complementary styles and who had different talents from their own. They were people who believed in both the arts and the sciences and what could be created when the two intersected. They were people who, first and foremost, believed in creating a good product. They knew that if a product was good enough, it would not need a lot of marketing. They were able to imagine products that people did not yet know they needed until they saw them. Some were intense, creative geniuses with driven personalities. Others were laid-back geeks and hippies who believed in building businesses that were anti-establishment and anti-hierarchical.

Trends that evolved as a result of technological advances were a recurring theme in this book. Changes came about not only due to creative genius, but also because of war and the necessity to build new weapons and security devices. The backing of venture capitalists played a large part in development, too. One trend that can be observed during the digital age was that devices kept getting smaller, more powerful, and less expensive. Another trend in the digital age was that devices, such as pocket transistor radios, cell phones, and digital music devices, were made for personal and portable use. One other transformation that came about was that no matter what devices were originally designed to be used for, people turned them into social devices. Radical differences in the culture of corporations in Silicon Valley were created as compared to the corporate culture of the east coast. These cultures made everyone into equals and did away with the hierarchy of power. There were no reserved parking spots, no dress codes, everyone had a similar cubicle, and engineers, designers, and scientists all mingled and collaborated together with flexible hours and schedules. The sharing of ideas was encouraged as each new innovation improved and built on the last. Ideas were exchanged from peer to peer and from generation to generation.

Some of the innovators in this book are discussed at great length while others are only briefly mentioned. At times, the rapid-fire listing of people who contributed to the digital age and the details of what their contributions were are overwhelming and confusing. It is difficult to keep straight the names with their matching accomplishments. It might have been better if fewer innovators had been written about more in-depth instead of briefly touching on so many.

Overall, this book is fascinating and informative to anyone with an interest in computers and other digital devices. It describes clearly how the digital revolution came about and how it has changed the world. It's all here, from the humble beginnings when visions of a machine for the future were held by Charles Babbage and Ada Lovelace to the creations of devices, such as the transistor, the micro-chip, the microprocessor, the mouse and keyboard, software, and the fully integrated personal computer to the success of entrepreneurs such as Bill Gates and Steve Jobs to the explosive changes that were brought about all over the world by the World Wide Web, the Internet, and social media.

~~~~ END OF INSTAREAD ~~~~

Lightning Source UK Ltd.
Milton Keynes UK
UKOW01f1151240717
305928UK00001B/54/P